100% UNOFFICIAL

100% UNOFFICIAL

100% UNOFFICIAL

100% UNOFFICIAL

100% UNOFFICIAL

**100%**
**UNOFFICIAL**

First published in Great Britain 2026 by 100% Unofficial, a part of Farshore
An imprint of HarperCollins*Publishers*
1 London Bridge Street, London SE1 9GF
www.farshore.co.uk

HarperCollins*Publishers*
Macken House, 39/40 Mayor Street Upper,
Dublin 1, D01 C9W8, Ireland

Written by Ben Wilson

This book is an original creation by Farshore


ISBN 978 0 00 881646 9
Printed in Romania
001

A CIP catalogue record for this title is available from the British Library.

100% UNOFFICIAL

# TAYLOR SWIFT

ANNUAL 2027

# CONTENTS

100% UNOFFICIAL

# THE FACT FILE OF A SHOWGIRL

**Your instant guide to all things Taylor Swift!**

## NAME:

Taylor Alison Swift

## BIRTHDAY:

13th December 1989

## STAR SIGN:

Sagittarius. That means she's honest, enthusiastic and generous. Her *Eras Tour* crew would agree. She gifted them $197 million!

## ANIMALS:

Taylor's trio of cats are almost as famous as her! Her feline friends are called Meredith Grey, Olivia Benson and Benjamin Button.

## HEIGHT:

1.80m (5'10")

Tay showing off her lucky 13 on her hand!

## BIRTHPLACE:

West Reading, Pennsylvania, USA

## FAVE COLOUR:

Nope, not Maroon. Or Red. Taylor told Ellen DeGeneres that her favourite colour is purple!

## NUMBER:

6–7… jokes! It is, of course, 13. It's T-Swift's birthday, she was born on Friday 13th, and her first album went gold in 13 weeks!

## BOOKS:

**'The Fate of Ophelia'** is inspired by the lead female character in *Hamlet*, by William Shakespeare. Taylor also refers to *The Great Gatsby* by F. Scott Fitzgerald in multiple songs!

Taylor is always scrumptious, but these fan cupcakes are next level!

Taylor posing with her idol – the one and only Tim McGraw!

## HOBBIES:

Collecting antiques, making snow globes and baking – especially cinnamon rolls!

## INFLUENCES:

Stevie Nicks, Joni Mitchell and The Chicks – who guested on **'Soon You'll Get Better'**. Plus, country icon Tim McGraw. He inspired the song **'Tim McGraw'** ... funny that!

## TV:

Historical drama *The Gilded Age* is a fave, as is Domhnall Gleeson's mockumentary series *The Paper*. Also, Meredith is named after a character from *Grey's Anatomy*!

## MOVIES:

Taylor loves *Pan's Labyrinth* and *The Shape of Water*. She also adored 2025 action-thriller *One Battle After Another*, starring Leonardo DiCaprio and Chase Infiniti.

## SPORTS:

She's a regular at Kansas City Chiefs matches to watch fiancé Travis Kelce. Tay also enjoys bowling and hockey.

## ACTING:

Taylor voiced Audrey in *The Lorax*, and has also appeared in *Cats*, *New Girl* and *CSI: Crime Scene Investigation*!

## FOOD:

Tay enjoys chicken tenders with what her *Eras Tour* page called "seemingly ranch" dressing. It became such a huge meme!

## HOLIDAY:

T-Swift grew up on a Christmas tree farm. In 2014, Taylor sent treats to 32 fans around the world to say Happy Swiftmas. Her friends even joke she's an elf!

TS celebrates a Travis touchdown with friend Brittany Mahomes!

# TAYLOR'S TIMELINE

**All the important dates in the life of our showgirl!**

Loving Taylor in her Red (Re-e-e-ed) dress!

## 1989

Taylor Alison Swift is born on 13th December in Reading, Pennsylvania, to Andrea and Scott. Her brother, Austin, completes the family three years later.

## 2006

Tay's first ever single and music video emerge. The song is called **'Tim McGraw'**, in honour of the country icon. Her debut album spends 24 weeks at the top of the country chart and is also a UK number one. Oh my (my my)!

## 2012

Two more Grammy Awards are added to the mantelpiece, while *Red* solidifies Taylor's status as the biggest pop star on the planet. It sees her edge towards a more pop-based sound, with tracks like **'I Knew You Were Trouble'**.

| 1989 | 2001 | 2006 | 2008 | 2010 | 2012 |
|---|---|---|---|---|---|

## 2001

Taylor starts writing songs after a computer repairman shows her the guitar chords C, D and G. Her first song is called **'Lucky You'**, while another – **'The Outside'** – eventually appears on her debut album, *Taylor Swift*!

The *Fearless Tour* rocks Madison Square Garden in New York!

## 2010

Taylor kicks off the year by picking up her first of four Album Of The Year Grammy Awards. She finishes off the 118 gigs on her *Fearless Tour* and releases *Speak Now*. It's a statement album, as every song is written on her own!

Tay's curl game was strong at the 52nd Grammys show!

## 2008

Album number two, *Fearless*, is preceded by the super catchy single **'Love Story'**. Its video, where Taylor woos a prince in an enchanted castle, turns her into a household name. Since then, it's been watched a staggering 800 million times!

Jack Antonoff understood the *1989* dress code in this cool bomber jacket.

Travis Kelce looking fine at the 2023 CMT Music Awards.

Us every time Taylor wore a new *Lover* bodysuit!

## 2013

Taylor is paired up with Fun guitarist Jack Antonoff on a song for the movie *One Chance*. They also record three tracks for her smash upcoming album, *1989*, become good mates and forge her most influential songwriting partnership!

## 2020

Following the release of *Lover* in 2019, the global *Lover Fest* tour sadly never happens, due to the world being in lockdown. Instead, Taylor releases two incredible folk albums: *folklore* and *evermore*.

## 2023

Taylor splits with English boyfriend Joe Alwyn after six years together, just as *The Eras Tour* gets underway. But she finds new love in NFL player Travis Kelce, while *Lover* favourite **'Cruel Summer'** finally catapults to number one!

## 2024

*The Eras Tour* enters its second year and ultimately becomes the most successful music tour in history. Not only that, but Tay also releases her pitch-perfect album, *The Tortured Poets Department*!

**2013 | 2017 | 2020 | 2022 | 2023 | 2024 | 2025**

## 2017

Tay spends the first half of the year lying low, other than the video for **'I Don't Wanna Live Forever'** with Zayn Malik. November, however, sees her roar back to top form with *Reputation*, a record laced with fury and vengeance!

## 2022

Album number ten arrives: the chilled-yet-glamorous *Midnights*. Its songs take over the entire US top ten! Tay also announces her biggest set of concerts ever, known as *The Ears Tour*. 2.4 million tickets are sold in one day!

## 2025

Taylor is not on tour, but as busy as ever! She buys back her master recordings, five years after they were sold. Travis proposes and Tay's twelfth album, *The Life of a Showgirl*, is yet another hit!

Swifties flock to the Rogers Center, as *The Eras Tour* hits Toronto.

Tay's *The Life of a Showgirl* shoot was her hottest yet!

# YOUR SWIFTIE JOURNAL

**You've got to know a bit about Taylor over the last four pages – now it's all about you!**

Taylor meets her fans at the 2012 MTV Music Awards!

**NAME:**

**AGE:**

**HOMETOWN:**

**FAVE COLOUR:**

**FAVE FOOD:**

**FAVE FILM:**

**FAVE TV SHOW:**

**FAVE BOOK:**

**FIRST TAYLOR ALBUM LISTENED TO:**

We all have heart eyes for the one and only TS!

Best believe these fans are still bejewelled!

## TOP 5 TAYLOR SONGS:

1:

2:

3:

4:

5:

## FAVE TAYLOR ALBUM:

## FAVE TAYLOR VIDEO:

## FAVE ERAS TOUR SONG:

## TOP 3 OTHER ARTISTS:

1:

2:

3:

## FAVE TAYLOR LYRICS:

A Taylor Swift pop-up shop? Umm, take our money!

ALBUM SPOTLIGHT

# THE LIFE OF A SHOWGIRL

## OPALITE GEM

*The Life of a Showgirl* (*TLOAS*) was Taylor's most anticipated album ever! She announced her twelfth album on Travis Kelce's podcast, *New Heights*, in August 2025. The project reunited her with Max Martin and Shellback, who produced *Red*, *1989* and *Reputation*. It's just as great as those classics!

### TOP TRIVIA

Release date: Oct 2025
All-time sales: 4 million
UK chart position: 1
US chart position: 1

## BESTSELLER

Lead single, **'The Fate of Ophelia'**, really kept it 100! It broke Spotify records for the most-streamed song in both one day (25.5 million) and one week (128 million). In the UK, it reached the top spot with 132,000 sales – the most of Tay's career!

## COOL COLLAB

Fans have been desperate for a collab with Sabrina Carpenter since she supported Taylor on *The Eras Tour*. We finally got that wish with title track **'The Life of a Showgirl'**. The album's finale blends the pair's singing styles perfectly and is surely the first of many Taylor-Sabrina duets!

Love and hugs for this iconic duo!

## TRACK FIVE

The fifth track on any Taylor album is always sure to be hand-picked as one of her most personal. Here, it's **'Eldest Daughter'**, a song about living up to the expectations of being a first child. It's a powerful look into her inner self – backed by a melody sure to give you goosebumps!

## YOUR *THE LIFE OF A SHOWGIRL* TOP 3 SONGS:

1. ........................................
2. ........................................
3. ........................................

## DID YOU KNOW?

T-Swift made the entire album during the second year of *The Eras Tour*. She dashed back and forth from the tour to Stockholm in Sweden to record with Martin and Shellback!

## SLEEPER SMASH

For the first week after release, the USA's top twelve songs were all from *TLOAS*! The laid-back **'Honey'** came in last, but it's since grown into a true fan fave. The song cleverly explains how a single word in the English language can go from hurtful to romantic!

*K-Pop Demon Hunters* brought some serious competition to Tay!

## CHART RIVALS

Since 2015, Adele's *25* album held the record for first-week album sales in the US, with 3.4 million. *TLOAS* overtook it, with 3.5 million! In the UK, the three-week run at number one of **'The Fate of Ophelia'** was ended by **'Golden'**, from *K-Pop Demon Hunters*.

How was T-Swift looking this glamorous on *The Eras Tour* AND dashing off to Sweden regularly to record *TLOAS*?!

# TOTALLY TAYLOR: TLOAS TRACK BY TRACK

**A guide to all twelve songs from our beloved *TS12*!**

## THE FATE OF OPHELIA

The first single from *The Life of a Showgirl* cleverly references Shakespeare! Ophelia is a character from *Hamlet*, who sadly dies after breaking up with the King. The dance to the song became a huge TikTok sensation!

We have a Shakespeare statue in London ... What about a Taylor statue?

Elizabeth Taylor looking glam at Cannes, back in 2002.

## ELIZABETH TAYLOR

This brilliant track is all about the rollercoaster ride of fame. Taylor compares herself to Elizabeth Taylor, a legendary actress whose personal life was constantly placed under the microscope by the media. It's impossible not to sing along (or cry your eyes violet)!

## FATHER FIGURE

This fan favourite cleverly samples a song by pop legend George Michael, also called **'Father Figure'**! It's about a paternal figure from Tay's past, who she outgrew. Most think it's Scott Borchetta, who signed Tay to her first record deal.

## OPALITE

The biggest toe-tapper on the album earned kind comparisons to the 1960s classic **'Be My Baby'**, by the Ronettes. It's about the lead character being rescued from sadness by an amazing partner – surely Taylor must be referring to her man, Travis. Give it another listen!

The amazing George Michael – really going for it!

## ELDEST DAUGHTER

Taylor only has one sibling: younger brother Austin. **'Eldest Daughter'** sees her delve into the expectations that come with being the oldest child, while battling self-doubt. It's another 'track five' insight into her human side.

## RUIN THE FRIENDSHIP

A beautiful song about regretting a friendship in which romantic temptations went ignored. Taylor laments the death of a high school pal, who she never kissed because it felt too risky. Best friend Abigail also gets a mention in this heartfelt tune.

## ACTUALLY ROMANTIC

Being at the top naturally attracts jealousy, and here Taylor writes a love letter to a celeb who apparently can't stop taking shots at her – both in private and public. Is it about a real person? That's up to you to decide!

Travis and Taylor cuddle up while watching the US Open tennis final!

## WI$H LI$T

A detailed look at the material things we want in modern society – and how they're all meaningless in comparison to true love. Taylor insists she'd trade her possessions for a simple life with Travis, in a house with a driveway and a basketball hoop.

## WOOD

The sauciest song Tay has ever written! **'Wood'** packs in the type of lyrical cheekiness that has made Sabrina Carpenter massive. Overcoming superstitions about love, Tay opens up about all the magical ways in which she's attracted to Travis.

## CANCELLED!

Thanks to social media, a single mistake in the public eye can lead to critics calling for you to be 'cancelled'. Taylor addresses the trend in this *Reputation*-era throwback, sticking up for pals who have endured internet negativity and scandal.

## HONEY

A brilliant mini-essay on the power of language. The song talks about how the word 'honey' was used cruelly for most of Tay's life – until she met Travis, when it became a positive nickname. Awww!

## THE LIFE OF A SHOWGIRL

In *Taylor Swift Annual 2026*, we predicted that *TS12* would feature a collab with Sabrina. This is it! Taylor lifts the lid on life offstage, via the tale of a fictional superstar called Kitty. Sabrina's parts are slick and smooth, finishing the album off in perfect showgirl style.

Sabrina warms up a spicy hot *Eras Tour* crowd in Melbourne.

# 13 ... BEST TLOAS MOMENTS

**The weeks before, during and after release were as awesome as the album itself! These were all the highlights ...**

Liverpool got a sneak peak of the *TLOAS* orange with this *1989* two-piece!

## 1 PODCAST REVEAL

Taylor announced the album in August 2025, on boyfriend Travis Kelce's podcast *New Heights*. The episode set a world record for the most live views for a podcast on YouTube, with an impressive 1.3 million!

## 2 COLOUR CRAZE

The orange colour used for the album sparked an online frenzy. Pinterest reported an 8,276% rise in searches for 'bold orange glitter' after Taylor's new artwork was revealed!

## 3 SABRINA HAPPINESS

Having been a devoted Swiftie for years, Sabrina Carpenter finally got to duet with Taylor on the title track. "I know someone who's freaking out and it's me," she wrote when the album's twelve song titles were unveiled on Instagram!

Sabrina is all smiles at the 2025 Brit Awards!

## 4 ENDLESS CHOICE

*TLOAS* was released on eighteen CD variants, eight vinyl editions and even a cassette. Target stores in the US opened at midnight to sell their exclusive – and completely gorgeous – 'Summertime Spritz' pink shimmer vinyl!

## 5 SIGNED BUNFIGHT

Autographed *The Life of a Showgirl* CDs dropped on Taylor's store on Friday 26th September. They sold out in under two minutes – and were soon selling on eBay for over £120!

## 6 STAR OF CINEMA

*The Official Release Party of a Showgirl* film hit cinemas for three days. It featured an intro from Taylor, explanations and lyric videos for each song, the amazing video for **'The Fate of Ophelia'** and an insight into the making of the MV!

Our fave trip to the cinema in 2025!

## 7 FATEFUL CLIP

Love for **'The Fate of Ophelia'** video continued long after the movie left cinemas. It had 109 million YouTube views in just under a month! We were soon rewarded with *TLOAS* video number two – the amazing '90s-style **'Opalite'**!

## 8 TV APPEARANCES

Tay did talk shows with Graham Norton and Seth Meyers to promote the album. On *The Tonight Show Starring Jimmy Fallon*, the audience sang along to every word of tracks like **'Opalite'**, even though it was only 24 hours old! Impressive.

We adored Tay's smart black dress worn on *The Graham Norton Show*.

## 9 RECORD BREAKER

*The Life of a Showgirl* smashed records! It became the most streamed album in one day on Amazon Music and went on to break Adele's record for the most first-week sales in America. On Spotify, it was the most pre-saved album ever. Tay-mazing!

## 10 MIAMI NICE

Turns out, an incredible tease for the album dropped long before it was released. Back in October 2024, Tay shared an Insta video of her in section A12 of her Miami show. *The Life of a Showgirl* was announced at precisely 12:12 … on 12th August!

## 11 EASTER EGGS

The Easter Eggs were scattered throughout the album's lyrics. Did you know that the opal from **'Opalite'** is Travis Kelce's birth stone? And Portofino, from **'Elizabeth Taylor'**, is where Richard Burton famously proposed to the actress in 1964? Well, you do now!

## 12 ACOUSTIC EXPANSION

Seven tracks were later added to form *The Acoustic Collection*! Especially wonderful are **'Eldest Daughter (Now You're Home Acoustic Version)'** and **'Ruin the Friendship (My Advice Version)'**.

Stay calm, but Tay is waving at YOU!

## 13 FAN FAVOURITE

Billboard polled fans on their best song from the album. **'Elizabeth Taylor'** came third with 10.1% of the vote, while **'Opalite'** was second with 19.5%. The winner, with 23.6%, was … **'The Fate Of Ophelia'**! No surprise!

## ALBUM SPOTLIGHT

# THE TORTURED POETS DEPARTMENT

## WORD PERFECT

**Lyrics were Taylor's therapy in this beautiful blend of pop, folk and piano majesty. The initial batch of sixteen songs were so powerful, that a couple of hours later Taylor added another fifteen tracks to form *The Anthology*! It's her longest album ever – over two hours of masterful melancholy.**

### TOP TRIVIA

**Release date: Apr 2024**
**All-time sales: 7 million**
**UK chart position: 1**
**US chart position: 1**

## BESTSELLER

Taylor teamed up with rapper Post Malone on **'Fortnight'**, and the pair were soon celebrating: the song overtook Mariah Carey's **'All I Want For Christmas Is You'** as the most-streamed song in one day on Spotify! The track also soared to number one in Canada, Malaysia and the USA.

## CHART RIVALS

A beaming Benson Boone rocks Texas!

**'Fortnight'** flew to number one on the UK singles chart ahead of 2024's biggest bangers. Also in the Top 20 that week were **'Beautiful Things'** by Benson Boone, **'Lose Control'** by Teddy Swims and Sabrina Carpenter's mega **'Espresso'**.

## SLEEPER SMASH

Initially, **'The Black Dog'** was a bonus track on one of four *The Tortured Poets Department* (*TTPD*) variants. It became so huge, that a pub in London, also called The Black Dog, became a shrine to Taylor! It even served up food like 'Opening Act Canapes' and 'Ophelia's Fate Pavlova'.

## ERAS EARWORM

*TTPD* songs were soon added to the setlist for the second year of *The Eras Tour*. **'Down Bad'** was a highlight, but even that was topped by an incredible five-minute blend of **'But Daddy I Love Him'** and **'So High School'**!

## COOL COLLAB

As if fans weren't excited enough by Taylor working with Florence + The Machine on **'Florida!!!'**, *The Eras Tour* sent things next level. On the final night at Wembley, with no prior warning, Florence appeared on stage for a stunning live duet!

## DID YOU KNOW?

Taylor wrote so many songs as she'd clearly been through a difficult period in her life. She described the album as "a data dump of everything I've thought, felt, experienced in two or three years" on the *New Heights* podcast!

## YOUR *THE TORTURED POETS DEPARTMENT* TOP 3 SONGS:

1. ........................................
2. ........................................
3. ........................................

## TRACK FIVE

**'So Long, London'** is the perfect callback to the joyful **'London Boy'**, from *Lover*. While the latter saw her fall in love with British actor Joe Alwyn, the *TTPD* song is a sad farewell to that relationship – and her brief romance with The 1975 singer Matty Healy.

100% UNOFFICIAL

The hair, the chains, the dress! Taylor completely oozed *TTPD*-era confidence at the 2023 Video Music Awards.

# TOTALLY TAYLOR: THE END OF AN ERA SERIES GUIDE

**Taylor wowed us all with her six-part *The End of an Era* Disney special! Here's your guide to every episode – and a certain live performance that dropped alongside it ...**

## WELCOME TO THE ERAS TOUR

Tay used those five iconic words to greet fans at the start of each night's show. Now this documentary series takes us behind the scenes! Episode one shows her choosing which tracks to perform and getting ready to have Ed Sheeran on stage for a Wembley duet!

Taylor and Ed perform a perfect acoustic set!

Episode two sees Florence join Tay at Wembley!

## MAGIC IN THE ERAS

It's the amazing Florence Welch's time to appear alongside Taylor. Their rehearsal footage of **'Florida!!!'** is unmissable! Charismatic dancers Kam and Amanda share their back stories, while Tay and her crew work hard to integrate *The Tortured Poets Department* songs into the set. The process is faultless, obvs!

## KISMET

The photography in this episode is just dreamy. Taylor shows off her hardcore choreography work – then gets soaked in an iconic Miami rain shower. Stylist Joseph tries out some new threads on Tay, including THE gold *Reputation* snake outfit that leaves fans screaming!

Everybody bow dramatically to Queen Taylor!

Sabrina calls Taylor ... from under the stage!

## REMEMBER THIS MOMENT

A sneak peek at the final *Eras Tour* show in Vancouver, with crew members reflecting on how it changed their lives. Taylor rehearses, and then nails, her final surprise set mash-up: an astonishing mix of **'Long Live'**, **'New Year's Day'** and **'The Manuscript'**!

## THANK YOU FOR THE LOVELY BOUQUET

T-Swift shares some insights into how she met Travis Kelce – and he makes an onstage appearance! It's new territory to him, but not for Sabrina Carpenter. She and Tay figure out how to surprise fans when performing together in New Orleans. Inevitably, the audience goes wild!

*The Eras Tour* truly was FIRE!

## MARJORIE

A must-see episode for *The Life of a Showgirl* fans! It shows Taylor recording the album in Sweden with experimental footage of **'The Fate of Ophelia'** and **'CANCELLED!'**. Taylor and her mum Andrea also fondly remember her gran Marjorie, and describe the emotions of performing that song.

The series offers glimpses into how Taylor makes music.

## PLUS A VERY SPECIAL BONUS ...

Alongside the series, Taylor unleashed *The Eras Tour: The Final Show*! It's a sequel to *The Eras Tour* movie, with new outfits and camera angles for favourites like **'Cruel Summer'** and **'illicit affairs'**. *The Tortured Poets Department* tracks are included, such as Tay's phenomenal **'But Daddy I Love Him'** / **'So High School'** crossover. The acoustic section blend of **'A Place in This World'** and **'New Romantics'** is bewitching, too!

"It's a cruel summer ... with YOU!" Yes, you!

ALBUM SPOTLIGHT

# MIDNIGHTS

## BEJEWELED BRILLIANCE

**Taylor's dreamiest pop album is all about what goes through our minds after dark! She revealed the track titles in a video series called *Midnights Mayhem With Me*, by pulling each one from a bingo machine! *Midnights* made her the first artist to win a Grammy for Album Of The Year four times.**

**TOP TRIVIA**

**Release date: Oct 2022**

**All-time sales: 4.3 million**

**UK chart position: 1**

**US chart position: 1**

Lenny Kravitz presents Tay with a deserved AMA!

## SLEEPER SMASH

**'Bigger Than The Whole Sky'** was one of seven tracks added to *Midnights: 3am Edition*. It's a farewell to a special person taken before their time. Many fans made the link to 2012 charity track **'Ronan'**, about a young Taylor fan who died of cancer.

## TRACK FIVE

*Midnights*' fifth track saw Tay reflecting thoughtfully on her own life. **'You're On Your Own, Kid'** is about finding peace in herself, and letting hope overcome loneliness. The line "and make the friendship bracelets" also sparked an *Eras Tour* swapping craze!

## YOUR *MIDNIGHTS* TOP 3 SONGS:

1. ..........
2. ..........
3. ..........

## DID YOU KNOW?

*The Batman* actress Zoe Kravitz is a close friend of Taylor's and helped write **'Lavender Haze'**. But her dad is a music legend too: American reggae-rock legend Lenny Kravitz!

## ERAS EARWORM

T-Swift finished her *Eras Tour* set with seven songs from *Midnights*. **'Lavender Haze'** and **'Bejeweled'** cemented their total 'bop' status, but **'Mastermind'** was the big winner – sending fans into a dreamlike state before the farewell fireworks of **'Karma'**.

## COOL COLLAB

A long-awaited duet with Lana Del Ray produced the beautiful **'Snow On The Beach'**, and there was an extra surprise in store. Tay teamed up with Ice Spice for a slay remix of **'Karma'** – and you definitely need to check out their super cool cosmic music video right now!

## BESTSELLER

**'Anti-Hero'** became a mental health anthem, as Tay wrote insightfully about her own insecurities. It was her ninth US number one and it racked up 17.4 million Spotify plays in one day. Spending an impressive eight weeks on top, it overtook **'Blank Space'** as her longest-running number one.

## CHART RIVALS

*Midnights*' biggest chart rival belonged to an ex! Harry Styles, who was the subject of tracks like **'Out Of The Woods'**, scored the top-selling UK album of the year with *Harry's House*. But in the US, Taylor topped her former flame, as well as Bad Bunny's *Un Verano Sin Ti*.

Taylor in this gorgeous gold sequin dress really hits different! The *Midnights* era was truly dreamy.

# 13 ... BEST MUSIC VIDEOS

**'The Fate of Ophelia' was an instant classic. These are the other contenders for Taylor's 'best vid ever' award ...**

Taylor, our lifesaver – complete with blue sequin swim cap!

Glammed-up in her diamond dress and matching black hair, Tay performs the TikTok-viral *Ophelia* dance moves.

## 1 BLANK SPACE

The most-watched video of Taylor's career sees her character go bananas smashing things up, after being cheated on by her rich boyfriend. It features a cameo appearance from her cat Meredith and has 3.7 billion YouTube views!

## 2 THE FATE OF OPHELIA

Those who saw *The Release Party of a Showgirl* in cinemas got a real treat: the reveal of this amazing video! Tay adopts a variety of glitzy showgirl personas, before reuniting her *Eras Tour* crew for a super glam hotel room party. Have you learnt the viral dance moves yet?

## 3 CARDIGAN

The wow factor here isn't glamour, but just how understated it all is. Tay looks back on a past relationship by moving from a cozy cabin, to a lush forest, to a piano floating in the sea. Thankfully, she's back in the cabin to finish!

Taylor plays a mossy piano while water pours from inside it!

## 4 OPALITE

While on *The Graham Norton Show*, Domhnall Gleeson joked that he'd love to be in a Taylor video. Within a week, she'd sent a script to him and all the other guests – including Graham. The vid broke Spotify's record for most views in a day!

Filmed in the Whitgift Centre in Croydon, UK, Taylor and Domhnall head down the escalator with their pretzels.

## 5 LOOK WHAT YOU MADE ME DO

Despite initial criticism, the video for this is now considered a classic! It begins with Tay rising from a grave and ends with her looking stunning, after killing off previous versions of herself!

## 6 YOU NEED TO CALM DOWN

This ended one of pop's most public feuds. Taylor fell out with Katy Perry after they both tried to hire the same backing dancers. At the end of this they made up – by Taylor dressing up as French fries and cuddling Katy in a burger costume!

Katy, Taylor and their iconic fast food friendship. Burger and chips, anyone?

## 7 I CAN DO IT WITH A BROKEN HEART

Taylor has made more creative videos, but this clip holds a special place in the heart of anyone lucky enough to have seen *The Eras Tour* live. It's four minutes of highlights and backstage footage that you'll want to watch again and again.

## 8 BAD BLOOD

At the height of Taylor's 'Girl Squad' era, she brought the full gang together for this action movie in miniature. They all got badass new names, too. Ellie Goulding was Destructa X, Selena Gomez was Arsyn … and Tay herself was Catastrophe!

This music video was explosive – literally! Taylor and her girl squad strut away from the fire.

## 9 BEJEWELED

Featuring Jack Antonoff, the Haim sisters and Hollywood icon Laura Dern, this is a modern-day take on *Cinderella*. Taylor escapes her family, but ghosts Jack's Prince Charming!

## 10 THE MAN

The fourth single from *Lover* saw Taylor direct one of her own videos for the first time. Not only that, she plays the lead man – literally! Doing so took over six hours in the make-up chair before every scene.

## 11 LOVE STORY

The clip that catapulted Taylor to super stardom. You've watched it a million times, but did you know it was filmed at Castle Gwynn in Tennessee? And that Taylor only learned the choreography just fifteen minutes before filming!

## 12 ANTI-HERO

Taylor's mental health anthem revealed all her insecurities and the video continues that theme. An anti-hero version of T-Swift warns the real one "everyone will betray you" – then a giant Taylor is too clumsy to enjoy a dinner party!

The gold ball gown, the curls – Tay's romantic look for this video was iconic!

## 13 ALL TOO WELL: THE SHORT FILM

The pinnacle of Tay's onscreen career. She wrote and directed the fifteen-minute tale of Sadie Sink's main character having her heart broken by Dylan O'Brien. Taylor herself appears at the climax. As does a certain red scarf …

## ALBUM SPOTLIGHT

# EVERMORE

## LOCKDOWN CLASSIC

**Taylor wrote *evermore* to convey the emotions she felt while isolating during the 2020 pandemic. It's a calm, laid-back album, and considered the little sister of *folklore*. Most of the record was penned and produced with Aaron Dessner, the songwriter and guitarist for cool American band The National.**

### TOP TRIVIA

**Release date: Dec 2020**
**All-time sales: 2.3 million**
**UK chart position: 1**
**US chart position: 1**

### BESTSELLER

Released as a single on the same day as *evermore*, **'willow'** went straight to number one, giving Tay her seventh chart-topper in the US. Across its first week of release, **'willow'** scored 59,000 sales, 12.3 million radio plays and 30 million streams!

### CHART RIVALS

Although *evermore* sold over one million copies, battling the likes of massive BTS album *Be*, it fell short of being the year's best-selling album in the US because of … *folklore*! The December release also stopped **'willow'** becoming number one – blame Mariah Carey's **'All I Want For Christmas Is You'**!

Marcus brought his trusty guitar to duet with Tay when *The Eras Tour* hit Vegas!

### TRACK FIVE

Somber piano ballad **'tolerate it'** was inspired by Daphne du Maurier's 1938 novel called *Rebecca*. The story is about a young woman who marries a wealthy older man, only to discover they're being haunted by the ghost of his previous wife!

### SLEEPER SMASH

It took a couple of years, but many fans now consider **'cowboy like me'** to be the album's best track. The gentle country-rock song charts two broken youngsters gradually falling in love, only for the narrator to have her heart broken. Marcus Mumford provides backing vocals. He even sang it on his own tour!

### COOL COLLAB

All-sister girl band Haim have been pals with Taylor since 2013, when they invited her to party after her split with Harry Styles! Seven years later, they finally teamed up on devilish whodunnit song **'no body, no crime'**. The trio even performed it live with Tay when *The Eras Tour* landed in California.

### YOUR *EVERMORE* TOP 3 SONGS:

1. ..........
2. ..........
3. ..........

### ERAS EARWORM

Some *evermore* tracks had to be cut from the second year of *The Eras Tour*, to make room for *The Tortured Poets Department* section. Fortunately, **'champagne problems'** stayed in the set, and was as glorious as ever. Taylor sang it from her piano, with fans going wild during the "lovely bride" bridge section!

### DID YOU KNOW?

The tracks **'champagne problems'**, **'coney island'** and **'evermore'** were all written with William Bowery. That's a fake name for Taylor's ex, Joe Alwyn!

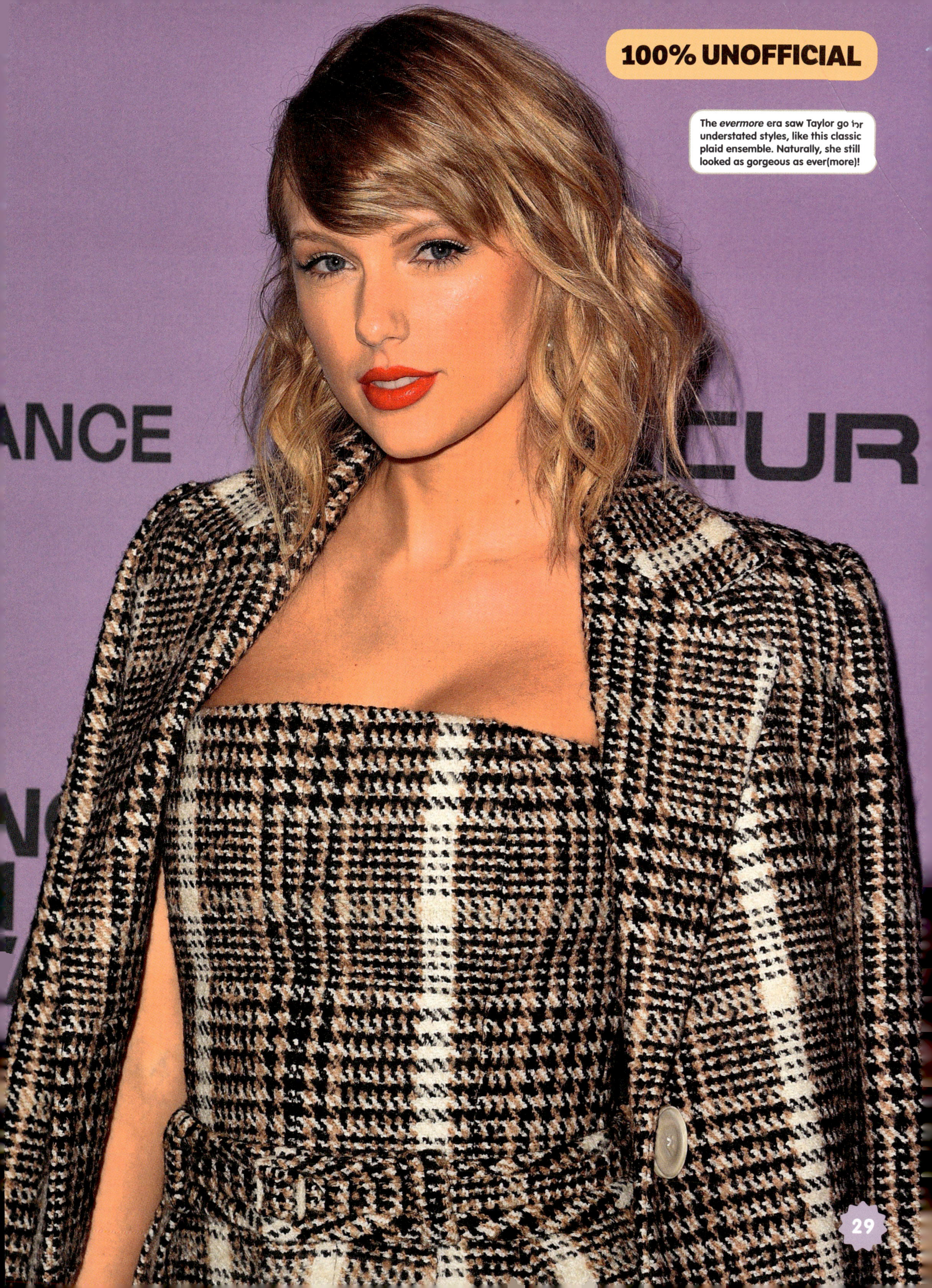


The *evermore* era saw Taylor go for understated styles, like this classic plaid ensemble. Naturally, she still looked as gorgeous as ever(more)!

# WHICH TAYLOR ERA ARE YOU?

**Every Swiftie has an era they feel matches their personality. But which is yours?**

**1**

**Which hairstyle are you rocking at the moment?**

**A** – The natural look
**B** – A full fringe
**C** – A smooth side parting
**D** – As glamorous as possible!

**2**

**What's your preferred music genre?**

**A** – Country
**B** – Pop
**C** – Acoustic
**D** – Rock

Tay looking utterly slay at the 2025 Grammy Awards.

**3**

**Which *Eras Tour* support act are you most likely to play on Spotify?**

**A** – Phoebe Bridgers
**B** – Paramore
**C** – Gracie Abrams
**D** – Sabrina Carpenter

**4**

**Which of these colours best suits your personality?**

**A** – Grey
**B** – Black
**C** – Purple
**D** – Orange

**5**

**What would be your ideal type of party with friends?**

**A** – Cosy sleepover
**B** – Noisy late night
**C** – Kitchen disco
**D** – Fancy dress glamfest

**6**

**Which accessory are you most likely to own?**

**A** – Poetry book
**B** – Snake bracelet
**C** – Red lipstick
**D** – Glitter pen

**7**

**Which of these album tracks do you know best?**

**A** – 'But Daddy I Love Him'
**B** – 'Call It What You Want'
**C** – 'Back to December'
**D** – 'Wi$h Li$t'

Now tally up your answers and put the number in each box!

A: B: C: D:

Which letter did you score most on? That one reveals your Taylor era ...

## A You are *The Tortured Poets Department*!

You are thoughtful, considerate and poetic, preferring a quiet evening in to a noisy night out! You're just as content in comfy PJs as a cutesy dress, and want your friends and family to be happy in life!

## B You are *Reputation*!

There's a fiery side to your character, but you use it to help out your mates and stand up for what you believe in. You enjoy embracing your emo side from time to time, and are obsessed with **'Look What You Made Me Do'**!

## C You are *Speak Now*!

You love your friends, but enjoy maintaining your independence too – after all, this was the album where Taylor penned every song on her own! **'Long Live'** is your anthem and **'Enchanted'** reminds you of your crush!

## D You are *The Life of a Showgirl*!

You haven't stopped playing Taylor's latest album since it came out and have seen the videos for **'The Fate of Ophelia'** and **'Opalite'** at least 50 times. Glitz and glamour are your morning priorities, even on a school day!

# ALBUM SPOTLIGHT

# FOLKLORE

## HAPPINESS IN EXILE

**The older sibling of *evermore* was a total surprise in 2020. Taylor recorded its low-key, folky songs while in quarantine, after the *Lover Fest* tour didn't happen. She announced *folklore* on 23rd July – and it came out at midnight! Lyrically, many fans reckon it's her strongest album.**

### TOP TRIVIA

**Release date: Jul 2020**
**All-time sales: 3.8 million**
**UK chart position: 1**
**US chart position: 1**

## COOL COLLAB

The deep voice of Justin Vernon from the band Bon Iver gave **'exile'** an incredibly unique sound. It's a tale of two ex-lovers sharing contrasting views of a break-up, which brilliantly switches between the male (Justin) and female (Tay) perspective.

It's *Eras Tour* Taylor (angry version)!

## ERAS EARWORM

Acoustic anthem **'illicit affairs'** was transformed by *The Eras Tour*. Taylor only sang the last two verses, but she belted them out on her knees, with anguish etched across her face. Fans adored it so much, they renamed it **'illicit affairs (angry version)'**!

## SLEEPER SMASH

Taylor was recently nominated for a spot in the Songwriters Hall of Fame. She picked five songs as the best in her repertoire. Joining **'All Too Well (10 Minute Version)'**, **'Blank Space'**, **'Love Story'** and **'Anti-Hero'** was *folklore* slow-burner **'the last great american dynasty'**!

## YOUR *FOLKLORE* TOP 3 SONGS:

1. ..........
2. ..........
3. ..........

## DID YOU KNOW?

Taylor styled her own hair, makeup and wardrobe for the 'cottagecore' album art. She's worked with its photographer, Beth Garrabrant, regularly ever since!

## TRACK FIVE

This album saw Taylor revel in telling beautiful stories, and **'my tears ricochet'** is a perfect example. It's the tale of a ghost who comes face-to-face with her ex – at her own funeral! The music is just as haunting as the lyrics. A spooky Swift classic.

## CHART RIVALS

Astonishingly, *folklore* went straight to number one in more than ten countries – including Australia, Estonia and Norway! In the US, it leapt over Harry Styles and The Weeknd to hit numero uno. Ellie Goulding's *Brightest Blue* was knocked off the top spot by *folklore* in the UK.

We'd still smile like Ellie if Taylor beat us to the top!

## BESTSELLER

On its first day of release, **'cardigan'** racked up 7.7 million Spotify streams in under 24 hours! It sold over 100,000 copies in one week between the UK and USA alone. In her home country, **'cardigan'** was Taylor's sixth number one single.

A demure Taylor at the 2020 Golden Globes. Little did we know that she would unleash two beautiful albums within twelve months!

# 13 ... THINGS YOU NEED TO KNOW ABOUT TRAVIS KELCE

**Taylor's soulmate had an eventful life, even before they got engaged! These are the best bits ...**

## 1 OHIO BOY

Travis Michael Kelce was born in Westland, Ohio, on 5th October 1989. If you know your Taylor albums, then you know that's the same year as Taylor – which is what gave us *1989*!

## 2 BROTHERLY LOVE

Travis has one brother, Jason. He's two years older and also plays American football. Together, they host the *New Heights* podcast, on which Taylor announced new album *The Life of a Showgirl*!

That's big bro Jason in the cap, hanging out with Trav.

## 3 EUROPEAN ANCESTRY

Travis is American, but his great grandparents emigrated to the US from Croatia! They lived in a breathtaking mountain region called Gorski Kotar.

## 4 HAIL TO THE CHIEF

Travis has spent his entire American football career with the Kansas City Chiefs. He's picked up dozens of individual awards, as well as helping the Chiefs win three Super Bowl championships!

## 5 GOLD RUSH

Travis went to the University of Cincinnati, which is over 200 years old. It was founded in 1819! Other famous graduates include Olympic gold medalist Mary Wineberg and Joseph Strauss – who built San Francisco's iconic Golden Gate Bridge!

Can't blame a guy for trying to hug THE Travis Kelce.

Big love for Travis from us Swifties!

## 6 LUCKY NUMBER

The number 87 has become legendary among Taylor fans, as Travis wears it on the field. He wears it in honour of his brother Jason, because he was born in 1987!

## 7 GENEROUS TO A T

Like Taylor, Travis is known for his philanthropy. He started the Eighty-Seven & Running Foundation in 2015 to help struggling teenagers from Ohio earn opportunities in education, business and athletics.

## 8 PROUD PARENTS

Mum Donna looking glamorous with her son!

Travis' dad, Ed, is a retired steel salesman, while mum Donna spent her career in banking. She's also appeared in TV shows, movies and was one of Glamour's Women Of The Year in 2024!

## 9 CHRISTMAS KINDNESS

Jason and Travis teamed up for a cover version of the Christmas hit, **'Fairytale Of New York'**. It was part of the 2023 album, *A Philly Special Christmas Special*, which raised $3 million for the treatment of poorly children in Philadelphia.

## 10 DIFFERENT HONEY

Acting is a new addition to Travis' CV. In *Happy Gilmore 2*, he plays a character called The Waiter. His funniest moment is being covered in honey by the legendary Bad Bunny!

## 11 MUSICAL INTERLUDE

The *Kelce Jam* is Travis' very own annual music festival! It started out in 2023, and has featured artists such as Machine Gun Kelly, Rick Ross and Lil Wayne.

## 12 BREADY FOR IT

Travis' fave food is Uncrustables. They're frozen, crust-free sandwiches with sweet treats inside – such as peanut butter and grape jelly! He said on *New Heights* that he eats them "probably more than I eat anything else in the world"! Yum.

Shelves stacked with Uncrustables ... Is this Travis' food cupboard?

Travis and Patrick Mahomes got to meet President Biden after winning the Super Bowl!

## 13 OFF TO FLORIDA!!!

As well as dating Taylor and hanging out with Chiefs pal Patrick Mahomes, Travis loves to play golf in his spare time. He also collects cars and spends time at his holiday home in Baldwin Park, Florida!

# ALBUM SPOTLIGHT

# LOVER

## LONDON BOY AFTERGLOW

**Can we go where she goes? Having been famed for her break-up songs, Taylor showed us that she could do an album focused on romance, too. *Lover* is all about Tay falling for her British boyfriend Joe Alwyn. Her artwork went pastel pink to match the happy Valentine vibe.**

### TOP TRIVIA

**Release date: Aug 2019**
**All-time sales: 5.6 million**
**UK chart position: 1**
**US chart position: 1**

## CHART RIVALS

Billie Eilish breakthrough *WHEN WE ALL FALL ASLEEP, WHERE DO WE GO* had a huge year in 2019. Even she couldn't compete with Taylor though! *Lover* was the best-selling album of the year – and it hit the top ten again in both 2023 and 2024!

## SLEEPER SMASH

It took four years – and a TikTok trend based around its incredible bridge – for **'Cruel Summer'** to be released as a single. The wait was worth it, though. In 2025, the second track on *Lover* screamed past 3 billion streams. Yes, 3 billion!

**"It's you and me" – Taylor to her iconic clamshells.**

## ERAS EARWORM

"It's been a long time coming but …" The phrase that changed 10.1 million lives. That's the total number who attended *The Eras Tour*, where Taylor kicked things off with that iconic line from **'Miss Americana & the Heart-Break Prince'**.

## COOL COLLAB

Taylor grew up idolising Texan country band the Dixie Chicks. She fulfilled a lifelong dream by having them sing on **'Soon You'll Get Better'**, about her mum suffering from cancer. It was one of their final recordings before changing their name to The Chicks!

## TRACK FIVE

**'The Archer'** holds a special place in many Swifties' hearts. Not only was it a standout from year one of *The Eras Tour*, but Taylor debuted it live in a one-off *City of Lover* concert to promote the album. It took place in Paris, and also made **'Cornelia Street'** a fan fave.

## DID YOU KNOW?

The sixteen-show *Lover Fest* tour was supposed to include a headline gig at the world-famous Glastonbury festival – but it was all sadly cancelled due to the 2020 pandemic.

**Brandon and Taylor are all smiles while performing 'ME!' In Las Vegas!**

## BEST SELLER

*Lover* was the last album where Taylor released singles ahead of the full record. The strategy worked for **'ME!'**, a nod-along duet with Panic! At The Disco frontman Brendon Urie. It sold 260,000 copies in its first week and broke the record for Alexa voice requests on Amazon!

## YOUR *LOVER* TOP 3 SONGS:

1. ..............................
2. ..............................
3. ..............................

Pinks, purples and pastels were the palette for Taylor's loved-up vibe. Here she looks radiant at the 2019 Billboard Music Awards.

# TOTALLY TAYLOR: THE TAY TO Z OF TAYLOR SWIFT

**From sunny August to Zzz (no, not sleep!), this is your alphabetical encyclopaedia of all things Tay Tay. Because 'hey kids, spelling is fun!'**

## A IS FOR AUGUST

Swifties celebrate this month because of the *folklore* love triangle formed by James, Betty and Augustine. Together the songs **'cardigan'**, **'betty'** and **'august'** tell a tale of teenage love – and heartbreak!

## B IS FOR BREAD

Taylor has become so obsessed with baking, that in addition to her famed cinnamon rolls, she's also a sourdough queen. One of her loaves even appears in the vid for **'The Fate of Ophelia'**!

## C IS FOR CRUEL SUMMER

*Lover*'s second track took four years to reach number one, after its spectacular bridge wowed fans on *The Eras Tour*. Soon after, *Rolling Stone* named it among the top 500 songs of all time!

## D IS FOR DEMOS

Tay made loads of songs in her early years that only ever appeared on unreleased demo discs for record companies. Titles include **'In The Pouring Rain'** and **'Never Fade'**. We'd love to hear them someday!

## E IS FOR ERAS TOUR

Spanning two years and 149 shows, Taylor's 2023–2024 tour is the biggest in music history. She performed 44 (or more!) songs every night, over 3.5 hours! BEST. SHOW. EVER.

**The ballgown, the guitar, the lights – like *The Eras Tour* itself, Taylor is the best of the best!**

## F IS FOR FOLKLORE

As well as being the most chill album of her career, it also spawned the delightful *folklore: the long pond studio sessions*. The Disney special features acoustic versions by Taylor, Jack Antonoff and Aaron Dessner, plus the stories behind each song!

## G IS FOR GRAMMY AWARDS

Tay is the only artist to have won Album Of The Year four times. She grabbed it for *Fearless* in 2010, *1989* in 2016, *folklore* in 2021 and *Midnights* in 2024.

**In 2010, Tay won four Grammys in one night!**

## H IS FOR HOME

Taylor owns properties across the US, including a swanky apartment in New York and a historic mansion in Rhode Island. It was once home to philanthropist Rebekah Harkness, who inspired **'the last great american dynasty'** from *folklore*!

Taylor's beautiful Rhode Island mansion, with the lawn mentioned in 'Who's Afraid of Little Old Me?'

## I IS FOR INSTAGRAM

Taylor has the 14th most followed Insta account and the eighth most-liked post ever. It was for her engagement reveal, which scored a whopping 37.6 million likes!

## J IS FOR JACK

Mr Antonoff is one of Taylor's main co-writers and producers, and a close friend. You can usually spot him on stage next to Tay when she goes up to grab her latest award!

Like Jack, we were in awe when Taylor won the Album Of The Year Grammy for *folklore*.

## K IS FOR KITTY

Kitty is the fictional star from **'The Life of a Showgirl'**. Taylor invented her as someone who is inspiring, but also warns wannabes about the perils of fame. Kitty is also the name of mum Andrea's Great Dane!

## L IS FOR LIZ ROSE

The country songstress helped propel Taylor to mega fame by co-writing hits like **'Love Story'**, **'You Belong With Me'** and **'All Too Well'**. Her daughter is also a country artist, called Caitlin Rose!

Smiley Liz Rose was inducted into the Songwriters Hall of Fame in 2023!

## M IS FOR MASTERS

The rights to the master recordings of Taylor's first six albums were controversially sold off in 2019. It took years of hard work, but she finally bought them back in 2025!

# TOTALLY TAYLOR: THE TAY TO Z OF TAYLOR SWIFT

Attention, Swifties! The T-shirt is back!

Swifties ready for *Eras Tour* magic at Wembley!

## N IS FOR NOT A LOT GOING ON AT THE MOMENT

Taylor's iconic slogan started out as a T-shirt in the **'22'** video and was then repeated by her on Instagram to fool fans shortly before she announced *folklore*!

## O IS FOR OPHELIA

Shakespeare's *Hamlet* character found a whole new audience thanks to the opening track on *The Life of a Showgirl* – with **'The Fate of Ophelia'** hogging the UK number one spot for weeks!

## P IS FOR POETRY

You've heard *The Tortured Poets Department* a million times by now, but Taylor also won a national poetry contest aged just ten years old! Her winning entry was called 'A Monster in My Closet'.

## Q IS FOR QUOTE

Taylor gives the best life advice. When collecting her degree (see 'U is for University'!), she told students that: "Hard things will happen to us. We will recover!"

## R IS FOR RED

The colour suits Taylor – and her man, too. Travis has worn it throughout his NFL career! *Red* is also the title of a certain supermassive album …

*Red* by name and nature – Tay stuns at the 2009 CMAs.

## S IS FOR SWIFTIES

Tay adores her fans, and they're totally committed in return. From swapping friendship bracelets at concerts to collecting her cardigans and snow globes, T-Swift definitely has the most devoted supporters in pop!

It's Travis rocking out at the CMT Music Awards!

## T IS FOR TRAVIS

Taylor dotes on her hunky soulmate. "He's just my favourite person I've ever met," she told *The Tonight Show Starring Jimmy Fallon*. "No offense to everyone else!"

## U IS FOR UNIVERSITY

Taylor received an honorary doctorate in fine arts from New York University in 2022 – and gave a speech to 19,000 students at the graduation ceremony!

Tay addresses the crowd during her graduation, at Yankee Stadium!

## V IS FOR VAULT

The sale of Taylor's masters had a bittersweet positive: it gave us *Taylor's Versions* of four albums, with unreleased 'From The Vault' tracks. Without them we might never have heard **'When Emma Falls In Love'** or **'You're Losing Me'**.

## W IS FOR WORTH

Our girl has amassed an incredible fortune and is worth close to $2 billion! She's the second richest pop star on the planet after Jay-Z. Rihanna and Selena Gomez also make the top ten. Go girls!

Selena and Taylor way, way, way, way back in 2008!

## X IS FOR XMAS

It's Taylor's favourite time of year, having grown up on a Christmas Tree farm. She even made a 20-minute festive mini album called *The Taylor Swift Holiday Collection*.

## Y IS FOR YOUTUBE

Taylor's videos have been just as important as her music and lyrics. Five songs are part of the 'billion views' club: **'Blank Space'**, **'Shake It Off'**, **'You Belong With Me'**, **'Bad Blood'** and **'Look What You Made Me Do'**!

'Look What You Made Me Do' has 1.5 billion views. Sip on that tea!

## Z IS FOR ZZZ

No, not sleep! But the three Zs that feature in one of Taylor's most memorable lyrics: "There's a dazzling haze, a mysterious way about you, dear." It's one of the main reasons that so many Swifties choose to have **'Lover'** as their wedding song!

## ALBUM SPOTLIGHT

# REPUTATION

## VENOMOUS RETURN

**The darkest album of Taylor's career is also her most misunderstood. After a year away from the limelight, Tay returned with a delicious fury that burned through tracks like 'Look What You Made Me Do' – but 'Gorgeous' and 'King Of My Heart' are truly wonderful love songs, too.**

### TOP TRIVIA

**Release date: Nov 2017**
**All-time sales: 4.1 million**
**UK chart position: 1**
**US chart position: 1**

All smiles for this talented duo!

### ERAS EARWORM

Taylor's *Reputation* outfit formed a symbolic image on *The Eras Tour*: a one-legged, one-armed black and red catsuit, with snake patterns! In this get-up, the vengeful stirrings of **'Don't Blame Me'** felt more powerful than ever before.

### COOL COLLAB

After half a decade of friendship, Taylor and Ed Sheeran followed up **'Everything Has Changed'** with the urgent and energetic **'End Game'**. Ed felt inspired after reconnecting with an old school friend, Cherry, at one of Taylor's parties. That friend is now his wife!

### SLEEPER SMASH

**'Getaway Car'** was released as a single in New Zealand and Australia – but it only reached number 96! Since then, it's become a beloved Swiftie favourite, after Taylor's Netflix documentary *Miss Americana* showed Tay and Jack Antonoff excitedly finishing its bridge together!

### CHART RIVALS

Taylor's long-awaited return knocked Sam Smith off the top spot in the US, with 1.2 million first-week sales. She had to settle for second place in global sales across the year, but she won't have been too sad: close pal Ed Sheeran had the top-selling album with ÷ *(Divide)*!

### YOUR *REPUTATION* TOP 3 SONGS:

1. ....................
2. ....................
3. ....................

### DID YOU KNOW?

Taylor blacked out all her social media before the album's release – then slowly started sharing eerie, silent videos of CGI snakes. And that's how the *Reputation* snake was born!

### BESTSELLER

These days, **'Look What You Made Me Do'** is considered a fan fave, but critics weren't so sure upon release. Thankfully, Taylor's fans lapped up her first single in ages, to the tune of 353,000 first-week sales!

Where can you find a job putting on Tay's boots for her?

### TRACK FIVE

After the angst of **'...Ready For It?'** and **'I Did Something Bad'**, Taylor changes pace with the dainty **'Delicate'**. It's the majestic tale of falling for someone new when you feel like the entire world has given up on you.

She'd not yet released 'mirrorball' – but Taylor truly dazzled like one in this incredible getup for the 2018 American Music Awards. Perfection!

SWIFTIES ACTIVITIES

# FRIENDSHIP BRACELETS ANAGRAMS

**Can you rearrange the letters to work out each Taylor song?**

1. VOLE TROYS
2. DANCETHEN
3. LURCE MUSERM
4. ALIEPOT
5. SI TI ROVE WON
6. EASHK TI FOF
7. AFTHER UGRIEF
8. HET CLABK OGD
9. TAYS TAYS TAYS

# CHIEFS MAZE

Can you reunite Taylor's number 13 with the 87 shirt in the middle?

# ALBUM SPOTLIGHT

# 1989

## THROWBACK STYLE

**Taylor named her fifth album after the year of her birth! It saw her leave country music behind and go pure pop, inspired by the music of the decade in which she was born. Even the packaging was 1980s themed, with Tay appearing in a collection of iconic polaroid photos!**

### TOP TRIVIA

**Release date: Oct 2014**
**TV release date: Oct 2023**
**All-time sales: 14.7 million**
**UK chart position: 1**
**US chart position: 1**

## SLEEPER SMASH

The spectacular **'Is It Over Now?'** was left off the original *1989* as it was too similar to **'Out Of The Woods'**. Nine years later, it soared to number one thanks to *1989 (Taylor's Version)* – and its incredible bridge went viral across TikTok and Insta!

## ERAS EARWORM

Having already been a smash single, **'Blank Space'** got even better on *The Eras Tour*. It featured Tay's dancers riding round on *Tron*-style bikes, as she led the crowd in a futuristic singalong!

Tay and Jack celebrate another win at the 2016 Grammy Awards!

## CHART RIVALS

In what would become a theme throughout their careers, close pal Ed Sheeran was Tay's biggest threat to *1989*. In the week it went to number one, Ed's album *X* was number two! George Ezra's *Wanted On Voyage* also hovered in the top ten.

## COOL COLLAB

While there were no duets on *1989*, a songwriting collab transformed Taylor's life. She teamed up with Jack Antonoff on **'Out Of The Woods'**, **'I Wish You Would'** and **'You Are in Love'**. A pen-sharing partnership was born – and a beautiful friendship!

## YOUR *1989* TOP 3 SONGS:

1. ........................................
2. ........................................
3. ........................................

## BESTSELLER

Nine million US radio listeners heard **'Shake It Off'** on the day it came out – and it's still the best-known song of Taylor's career. It was one of the biggest singles of the decade; with so many sales, it was certified 'diamond'!

Our girl hits the Golden Globes in the build up to *1989*.

## DID YOU KNOW?

Tay worked with songwriting legend Diane Warren on **'Say Don't Go'** – but Diane didn't hear the finished track until the release of *1989 (TV)*, nearly a decade later!

## TRACK FIVE

**'All You Had To Do Was Stay'** is faster paced than Taylor's usual track five songs, but as ever, it's laced with personal feelings. The heartbreak anthem is about being left by a partner she'd gradually opened up to. Awww!

The *1989 Tour* spanned 85 shows, starting in Tokyo and ending in Melbourne. Here, Taylor wows Shanghai in an iconic white two-piece outfit!

# 13 ... TOP SWIFT SQUAD BESTIES

**Tay's Swift Squad has evolved since her besties appeared in 'Bad Blood'. These are the closest people in her life right now ...**

1

## ANDREA SWIFT

Taylor's mum has featured in several songs, most recently in **'Opalite'**. Taylor also wrote **'Soon You'll Get Better'** about her mum's battle with cancer. Andrea gets on well with Travis' mum Donna, too. Phew!

2

## TRAVIS KELCE

Our lady met her future smiley husband on *The Eras Tour* and they've been smitten ever since. *The Tortured Poets Department* may have been a break-up album, but **'So High School'** was an excitable love letter to her new man.

3

## ABIGAIL ANDERSON

Taylor wrote **'Fifteen'** for her pal Abigail back at Henderson High School in Tennessee. The pair are still super close, two decades later. This is the Abigail who Taylor refers to in **'Ruin the Friendship'**!

4

## SELENA GOMEZ

This pop-tastic pair first met in 2008 when they were dating different Jonas Brothers. Their hangouts regularly appear on Selena's Insta and Taylor gave a speech at Selena's wedding in September 2025.

5

## JACK ANTONOFF

Bleachers guitarist Jack has played a massive part in Taylor's world domination. He's co-written and produced favourites like **'Out Of The Woods'** and **'Getaway Car'**, and become a true bestie along the way.

The ever-glamorous Selena performed her song 'Good For You' with Tay on the *1989 Tour*, back in 2015!

6

## SABRINA CARPENTER

Many consider Sabrina the heir to Taylor's queen of pop throne – and now they're super close. Sabrina was a popular support act on *The Eras Tour* and the only one chosen for a collab on *The Life of a Showgirl*.

Always super cool and laid-back, Haim formed in 2007 and they've toured with Rihanna and The Killers!

7

## HAIM

Tay's friendship with the sibling trio is so strong, she calls herself the fourth Haim sister! They collaborated on **'no body, no crime'** and played Tay's wicked stepsisters in the vid for **'Bejeweled'**.

8

## KELEIGH TELLER

Keleigh appeared in the video for **'I Bet You Think About Me'** with her husband Miles Teller. Keleigh and Tay became – quite literally! – swift friends. She even went as Taylor's date for the Golden Globes in 2024.

9

## BRITTANY MAHOMES

Brittany is an ex-footballer and the wife of Travis Kelce's teammate Patrick Mahomes, who has guided the Chiefs to three NFL Championships. Brittany and Taylor often watch their matches together – and go out for dinner afterwards!

10

## ED SHEERAN

As well as collaborating on **'Everything Has Changed'** and **'End Game'**, Ed has popped up on Taylor's tours. She found it hard to tell him about her engagement to Travis, as he doesn't use a mobile phone!

The calm and cool Ed was listed as one of the world's 100 most influential people in 2025 by TIME magazine!

11

## SOPHIE TURNER

Taylor befriended Sansa from *Game of Thrones* when they appeared on *The Graham Norton Show* in 2017. They're so close, that Sophie and her children stayed at Taylor's NYC apartment following the end of her marriage.

12

## ICE SPICE

The cooler-than-cool rapper teamed up for a perfect **'Karma'** remix and was spotted partying with Taylor at the Super Bowl. Let's hope for another collab on *TS13*!

13

## ALYSON HANNIGAN

The Buffy star is such a massive Swiftie that Tay sent her a special edition of *The Life of a Showgirl*. As well as the album, she got a sweatshirt, shorts and hand-written letter!

# ALBUM SPOTLIGHT

# RED

## COLOUR-CODED

**Taylor's final country album proved that no one could write about breakups quite like her. It found triumph through heartbreak, mixing tearjerkers like 'All Too Well' with the catchy 'Starlight' and 'Holy Ground'. Over a decade later, it still sounds just as glorious!**

### TOP TRIVIA

**Release date: Oct 2012**
**TV release date: Nov 2021**
**All-time sales: 7.3 million**
**UK chart position: 1**
**US chart position: 1**

## BESTSELLER

**'We Are Never Ever Getting Back Together'** was released as a single two months ahead of *Red*. With 623,000 copies sold in a week, it became the fastest-selling single by a female artist in the history of the USA's music chart!

## ERAS EARWORM

Not only did **'22'** get the crowd singing along with glee, but it also provided a nightly highlight. Towards the end of the song, Taylor placed her black hat on the head of a very lucky audience member! That's a lot of hats!

That legendary T-shirt – onstage in Arlington, Texas!

## TRACK FIVE

Many fans feel **'All Too Well'** is the best song of Tay's career. It was a cult hit upon first release and gained more love when Taylor's Version emerged nine years later. At ten minutes and thirteen seconds, it's the USA's longest number one ever!

Taylor looks all too well all the time!

## SLEEPER SMASH

Country ballad **'Better Man'** was an immediate favourite when *Red (Taylor's Version)* was released in 2021. Tay actually wrote it for the original album, but gave it to the group Little Big Town – who took it to number one!

## YOUR *RED* TOP 3:

1. ..............................
2. ..............................
3. ..............................

## CHART RIVALS

Across the globe, 2012 was a triumphant year for female solo stars. Other huge sellers alongside *Red* included *21* from Adele, Lana Del Rey's *Born To Die* and *Our Version Of Events* by Emeli Sandé.

## COOL COLLAB

Deep cut **'The Last Time'** is one of the most underrated duets of Taylor's career. She wrote and recorded it with Snow Patrol frontman Gary Lightbody. They even teamed up to perform it live on *The X Factor* in November 2013!

## DID YOU KNOW?

The song **'Run'**, from *Red (Taylor's Version)*, was written with Ed Sheeran on the same day as **'Everything Has Changed'**!

Taylor promoting the album at the 2013 CMT Awards. But what song did she choose to perform? It had to be *'Red'*!

# TOTALLY TAYLOR: EVERY ERA EXPLAINED

**Taylor is the queen of reinvention, evolving her outfits, hair and make-up for each new album release. Here's a look back at all her unforgettable eras!**

## TAYLOR SWIFT

16-year-old Tay was as famous for her gorgeous curls as her country-themed debut album! She completed the natural look with flowing dresses and understated jewellery.

## FEARLESS

Taylor's golden era wasn't all about that single colour. She also rocked our world with badass black cowboy boots! Gorgeous tasseled dresses became a wardrobe staple too.

## SPEAK NOW

Mature make-up and eyeliner traced Taylor's path from talented teen to powerful woman. As for her outfits, this will forever be known as the purple era. **'Enchanted'**, indeed!

## RED

Colours were becoming a fashion hook for Tay, and this era needs little explanation! Her outfits, lipstick and artwork all stuck to red – apart from a very famous white T-shirt …

## 1989

A coastal theme accompanied Taylor's throwback pop record. Seagulls adorned her sweaters and shirts, while Tay debuted blue skirts and sparkly jackets. Oh, and a blonde bob!

## REPUTATION

There will be no explanation, just … skull rings, snake bracelets, smoky eyeliner, knee boots and black catsuits, actually. What a rebellious era this was!

## LOVER

Head over heels with Joe Alwyn, Taylor switched it up with butterflies, lollipops and alllll the pink. Even her footwear changed, as simple sandals matched her laid-back, loved-up vibe.

## FOLKLORE & EVERMORE

Lockdown brought two folky albums and a cottage-core makeover. That meant lumberjack shirts, minimal make-up and braided hair – as perfected for the *evermore* cover!

## MIDNIGHTS

Ohhhh yes. *Midnights* dropped shortly before *The Eras Tour* and Taylor was back in full glam mode – with a 1970s twist. We're talking straightened locks, vintage corduroy galore and bejwelled, sequin-heavy performances!

## THE TORTURED POETS DEPARTMENT

Black-and-white imagery was a natural fit with Taylor's wordiest, most vulnerable record. Oxford heels, corsets and lyric-covered dresses oozed confidence through the heartbreak.

## THE LIFE OF A SHOWGIRL

With a title like that, Tay had to unleash all the glitz and glamour – this time in orange! An array of looks for **'The Fate of Ophelia'** video showcased Tay at her most confident and fashionable!

## ALBUM SPOTLIGHT

# SPEAK NOW

## PERFECTLY PURPLE

**The third album of Taylor's career is the only record she's written all on her own! It showcased her divine ability to summarise the ups and downs of relationships by mixing country melodies with pop choruses. Oh, and it gave us the iconic 'Long Live' and 'Haunted'!**

### TOP TRIVIA

**Release date: Oct 2010**
**TV release date: Jul 2023**
**All-time sales: 6.5 million**
**UK chart position: 1**
**US chart position: 1**

## ERAS EARWORM

**'Enchanted'** was the only song from *Speak Now* to feature on every night of *The Eras Tour* – where it regularly stole the show. Tay glammed it up in a ballgown as her dancers put on a truly flawless ballet display!

## TRACK FIVE

**'Dear John'** might not get mentioned as often as other track fives, but it's just as powerful! The title references the type of letter written by a man to his partner, casually letting them know that the relationship is over.

Taylor and, um, Taylor – hanging out in 2012!

## CHART RIVALS

Katy Perry classic *Teenage Dream* was 2010's best-selling album, with *Speak Now* finishing a respectable fourth. We doubt Taylor's that bothered. She's the only artist ever to have a year's best-selling album eight times!

CMT glory for Taylor, at the tender age of 18!

## SLEEPER SMASH

**'Back To December'** was the second single from the album and love for it has grown over the years. It's a song Taylor wrote for her ex, Taylor Lautner, about the mistakes she made when they were together. They're good friends now!

## BESTSELLER

Surprisingly, none of the songs from *Speak Now* hit number one in the US – but **'Mine'** came closest, peaking at number three. It sold over 2.3 million copies and grabbed Video of the Year at the CMT Music Awards!

## COOL COLLAB

Writing the album solo meant there were no collabs on the original *Speak Now*. That changed for *Taylor's Version*, as she teamed up with Hayley Williams from Paramore on the gentle **'Castles Crumbling'**!

## DID YOU KNOW?

Brazilian singer Paula Fernandes was allowed to re-record **'Long Live'** in her native tongue of Portuguese to promote Taylor's *Speak Now World Tour – Live* DVD!

## YOUR *SPEAK NOW* TOP 3 SONGS:

1. ..............................
2. ..............................
3. ..............................

Our girl out and about to promote *Speak Now*. She announced the album on a now-long-gone live service called Ustream!

# DESIGN YOUR TS13 COVER

**What's your dream sound for Taylor's next album? Pure pop, a country throwback or something else? Bring it to life by designing your own cover!**

What will you call the album?

Are you going glittery or pared back?

What colour scheme will you choose?

# 2020s WORDSEARCH

**Taylor's been at her pinnacle this decade – so can you find all 13 favourite songs from her three most recent albums?**

| | | | | | | | | | | | | | |
|---|---|---|---|---|---|---|---|---|---|---|---|---|---|
| V | L | H | E | O | N | S | T | Q | B | E | J | B | O |
| D | D | A | R | F | P | Y | G | R | G | L | R | E | P |
| S | O | H | I | G | H | S | C | H | O | O | L | J | A |
| Q | W | W | G | M | I | P | N | D | S | M | Q | E | L |
| U | I | G | N | B | E | H | A | Q | W | L | T | W | I |
| P | S | J | E | B | V | T | R | O | C | J | J | E | T |
| R | H | A | K | L | A | W | O | F | Y | U | O | L | E |
| E | L | D | E | S | T | D | A | U | G | H | T | E | R |
| N | I | J | I | M | M | G | A | D | F | Y | S | D | E |
| T | S | N | B | K | Z | A | Y | B | N | R | O | W | C |
| O | T | F | A | O | F | O | R | T | N | I | G | H | T |
| S | P | R | A | Z | V | C | T | O | C | B | E | P | D |
| K | M | R | C | L | A | R | A | B | O | W | V | Z | A |
| A | N | T | I | H | E | R | O | H | O | N | N | D | H |

## MIDNIGHTS

KARMA
BEJEWELED
ANTI-HERO
MAROON

## TTPD

SO HIGH SCHOOL
LOML
DOWN BAD
CLARA BOW
FORTNIGHT

## TLOAS

WOOD
ELDEST DAUGHTER
OPALITE
WISH LIST

# ALBUM SPOTLIGHT

# FEARLESS

## TAY TAY GOES GOLD

**Taylor chose the right colour for *Fearless*. It hoovered up trophies and is the most successful country album ever! She won Album Of The Year at both the Country Music Association Awards and the Grammy Awards – one of four Grammys she collected in 2010!**

### TOP TRIVIA

**Release date: Nov 2008**
**TV release date: Apr 2021**
**All-time sales: 12 million**
**UK chart position: 1**
**US chart position: 1**

## CHART RIVALS

With **'Love Story'**, Taylor was denied her first UK number one single by Kelly Clarkson's brilliant **'My Life Would Suck Without You'**! It was a different story Down Under – Australian fans propelled it to the top, dethroning **'Right Round'** by Flo Rida!

Winning over new fans at the 2008 Stagecoach Country Music Festival!

## BEST SELLER

**'Love Story'** transformed Taylor from country starlet to worldwide superstar. Not only has the song sold more than 12 million copies, but she's performed it on tour more than any other song – at least 640 times!

## COOL COLLAB

Colbie Caillat teamed up with Tay on **'Breathe'** and happily re-recorded her vocals for *Fearless (Taylor's Version)* – she then released her own album of duets in 2025. *The Eras Tour* guest Maren Morris appears on the track **'Fallin' For You'**!

## YOUR *FEARLESS* TOP 3 SONGS:

1. ....................
2. ....................
3. ....................

## SLEEPER SMASH

**'Change'** is rarely performed by Taylor these days, but it's among the album's catchiest songs. You have to watch its fresh-faced video! The track came out three months ahead of *Fearless*, in support of the USA's 2008 Olympics team!

## ERAS EARWORM

**'You Belong With Me'** has been just as key to Taylor's glittering career as **'Love Story'**. This was obvious on *The Eras Tour*, where fans bounced along to every word of both songs with wide smiles and endless energy! Yes, we are OK!

## TRACK FIVE

**'White Horse'** was co-written with Liz Rose, who also co-wrote **'All Too Well'**. It's about the same boy as **'Love Story'**, who Taylor never got together with! At the 2010 Grammys, **'White Horse'** won Best Country Song and Best Female Country Vocal Performance.

With her Grammys for *Fearless* and 'White Horse'!

## DID YOU KNOW?

Taylor released the *Beautiful Eyes* EP four months before *Fearless*. It featured two new songs called **'I Heart?'** and … **'Beautiful Eyes'**!

The *Fearless Tour* lands in New York's legendary Madison Square Garden. 'You Belong With Me' kicked off the show, while the last song was 'Should've Said No'!

# 13 ... BEST TAYLOR EASTER EGGS

**Tay adores hiding secret treats in her songs, videos and artwork! These are the sneakiest, cheekiest teases of her career ...**

## 1 CAPITAL LETTERS

TS began playing around with Easter Eggs when she was making her first album, aged 15. "I decided to encode the lyrics with hidden messages using capital letters," she told *The Washington Post*. "That's how it started!"

## 2 PLAYFUL NAILS

The themes for *Reputation* and *Lover* were drastically different. But Taylor actually told us the change from vixen black to loved-up pink was coming by painting her nails pastel colours in a Spotify video for **'Delicate'**!

## 3 LIFT BUTTONS

The elevator numbers in the video for **'Bejweled'** got fans flustered. 13 was purple, which everyone reckoned was a tease for *Speak Now (Taylor's Version)*. And right they were!

## 4 NO SCOOTERS

The man who sold Taylor's masters is called Scooter Braun. He got a deserved swipe from Taylor in the video for **'The Man'**, with a 'no scooters' sign on the subway!

So many Taylor Easter Eggs! 13th Street Station, karma, 1989 and the 'missing' sign (for her 'stolen' masters).

Can you match the lift numbers with the corresponding Taylor albums? Use the colours to help!

## 5 ORANGE DOOR

At the very end of the final show of *The Eras Tour*, Taylor's exit was different – she walked through an orange door. It mystified Swifties for months ... until she revealed the main colour for *The Life of a Showgirl*!

## 6 1989 CALLBACKS

Tay references her birth year wherever she can. 1989 is on a number plate in *All Too Well: The Short Film*, a bridge in **'I Can See You'** and the unforgettable intro to *The Eras Tour*!

Taylor and her dancers all in red cabaret-style costumes. Look super closely – there's Travis in the top left corner!

## 7 OPHELIA VIDEO

Watch **'The Fate of Ophelia'** for an Easter Egg bonanza! Look out for the song's title in the lobby, Kitty's name on a clapboard and a photo of Travis in Tay's dressing room!

## 8 WILLOW INTRO

Swifties consider *folklore* and *evermore* to be sister albums. Clearly Tay does too. The video for **'willow'** cleverly runs on directly from the end of the video for **'cardigan'**!

Taylor drying off in her 'cardigan' cabin, at the start of 'willow'.

## 9 AWARDS HAIR

Taylor weirdly turned her back to the cameras to show off braided hair at the 2020 AMA Awards. Except it wasn't weird … but an Easter Egg for the upcoming *evermore* album cover!

## 10 ELLEN'S TATTOO

The video for **'You Need To Calm Down'** emerged two months before *Lover* and saw TV presenter Ellen DeGeneres getting a tattoo with the words **'Cruel Summer'**!

## 11 JAKE LYON

There's a mystery actor listed in the *All Too Well (The Short Movie)* credits as Jake Lyon – and everyone assumes the song is about Jake Gyllenhall. Jake Lyon = Jake Lying?!

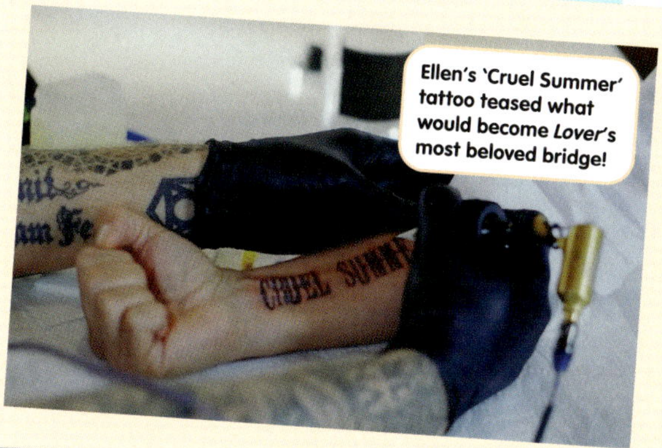

Ellen's 'Cruel Summer' tattoo teased what would become *Lover's* most beloved bridge!

## 12 BLUE GOWNS

Fans sussed Taylor was up to something when she wore blue dresses for the final Los Angeles leg of *The Eras Tour*. Sure enough, Taylor announced *1989 (Taylor's Version)* that night!

Taylor teasing *The Life of a Showgirl* in her sparkly orange and green two-piece. She's a true genius!

## 13 ANTI-HERO DOUBLE

The **'Anti-Hero'** vid features a scene where a Taylor wearing orange and green stares down a Taylor in all white. Fans suspect it's a reference to switching eras from *TTPD* to *The Life of a Showgirl*!

## ALBUM SPOTLIGHT

# TAYLOR SWIFT

### DEBUT DELIGHTS

**Incredibly, Taylor's debut album only reached number 81 in the UK! But its success on the American country charts suggested a historic career was on the way. 'Tim McGraw' was her first ever single, named after Taylor's music icon.**

### TOP TRIVIA

**Release date: Oct 2006**
**All-time sales: 9.1 million**
**UK chart position: 81**
**US chart position: 5**

Tay singing with one of her all-time idols: the actual Tim McGraw!

### BESTSELLER

**'Our Song'** was the third single off the album and Taylor's first massive hit. It flew to number one on both the Canadian and USA country charts, eventually racking up more than 5 million sales worldwide!

### COOL COLLAB

It was a bit early in Taylor's career for guest stars – but she penned deluxe edition track **'A Perfectly Good Heart'** with Troy Verges. He's a country writer who has crafted tunes for Tim McGraw, Celine Dion and Gwyneth Paltrow!

### SLEEPER SMASH

**'Should've Said No'** still rocks 20 years later, but it nearly missed out! Taylor wrote it two days before finishing the album, working with producer Nathan Chapman overnight to make sure it was completed. It was worth it, guys!

### CHART RIVALS

Like Taylor, the biggest selling album of 2006 is still influencing pop culture. The *High School Musical* soundtrack gave us Zac Efron, Ashley Tisdale and spin-off series *High School Musical: The Musical* – AKA Olivia Rodrigo's big break!

### DID YOU KNOW?

On the same day that Taylor announced she'd reclaimed her masters, our queen of pop also confirmed *Taylor Swift (Taylor's Version)* was complete! Alas, she didn't give a release date …

### ERAS EARWORM

*Taylor Swift* was the only era not to get its own slot on *The Eras Tour*. Nooo! Thankfully, every track made a secret song appearance – with both **'Our Song'** and **'Teardrops On My Guitar'** being played twice.

### YOUR *TAYLOR SWIFT* TOP 3 SONGS:

1. ........................................
2. ........................................
3. ........................................

### TRACK FIVE

Taylor's plan of memorable track fives hadn't started out at this point – but **'Cold As You'** fit that template anyway! She's said it's her favourite from the album, as it's about realising that you no longer have to make excuses for an ex's past behaviour. Slay, Tay!

One of Taylor's first ever shoots, in Nashville, Tennessee – aged 16. She'd soon turn from princess of country into queen of pop!

# TOTALLY TAYLOR: TS BY NUMBERS

**All the must-know stats and figures from Taylor's phenomenal career!**

## TAYLOR'S HAD SIX NUMBER ONE SINGLES IN THE UK ...

**'Look What You Made Me Do'**
**'Anti-Hero'**
**'Is It Over Now?' (Taylor's Version)**
**'Fortnight'**
**'The Fate of Ophelia'**
**'Opalite'**

## 83

Performances of **'The Archer'** and **'tolerate it'** on *The Eras Tour*, before they were swapped out for *The Tortured Poets Department*!

**Taylor gets even more gorgeous with age! Here she's arriving at the world premier of *The Eras Tour* movie, in LA.**

## 13

Not just Taylor's lucky number – but also the number of her next album. We cannot, cannot, cannot wait!

## 24

Weeks that *Taylor Swift* held on to the number one spot on the USA Country Albums chart – despite her being just 16!

## 2023

The year when 'Swiftie' was officially added to the *Oxford English Dictionary*. It's defined as "An enthusiastic fan of the singer Taylor Swift". Hello, you!

# 46

Months between the album release of *Lover* and the single release of **'Cruel Summer'**. Despite the wait, it flew to number one!

# 2

Loaves of bread Taylor baked Jimmy Fallon before her appearance on *The Tonight Show* – but she begged him not to take them out on stage!

# 41

Minutes of music on *The Life of a Showgirl* – the shortest album of her career!

# 73

Questions answered by Taylor in a 2016 *Vogue* interview. She revealed she has double-jointed elbows and her brother calls her 'Teffy'!

Taylor bedazzling Chinese fans on the *1989 Tour*, with songs like 'New Romantics' and 'Clean'!

# 118

Gigs on the *Fearless Tour* – Taylor's first ever. In comparison, *The Eras Tour* ran for 149 dates!

## MOST PLAYED TOUR SONGS

1: **'Love Story'** – 641
2: **'You Belong With Me'** – 532
3: **'Our Song'** – 431
4: **'Fearless'** – 416
5: **'We Are Never Ever Getting Back Together'** – 368

# THE COLOURING OF A SHOWGIRL

**Colour the items, then write down the name of each *TLOAS* song using the clues!**

**CLUE:** Heard you calling on this!
**YOUR ANSWER:**

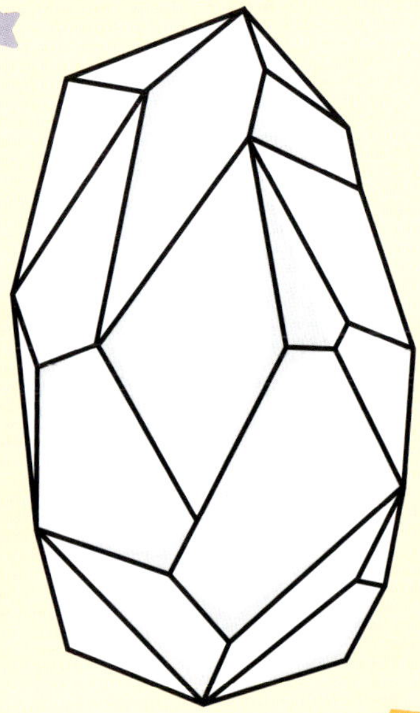

**CLUE:** A gem made in the lightning strikes.
**YOUR ANSWER:**

**CLUE:** You can eat it if you want!
**YOUR ANSWER:**

**CLUE:** These lovely flowers belong to Kitty.
**YOUR ANSWER:**

# CREATE YOUR OWN SETLIST!

*The Eras Tour* may be over, but Taylor will be back out on the road someday. Choose your fave tracks to make your own dream live set. We've even included space for secret songs!

1: ..........

2: ..........

3: ..........

4: ..........

5: ..........

6: ..........

7: ..........

8: ..........

9: ..........

10: ..........

11: ..........

12: ..........

13: ..........

14: ..........

15: ..........

16: (Surprise duet) ..........

17: (Acoustic) ..........

18: (Piano) ..........

19: (Encore) ..........

20: (Encore) ..........

# ANSWERS:

## P.44

1. LOVE STORY
2. ENCHANTED
3. CRUEL SUMMER
4. OPALITE
5. IS IT OVER NOW
6. SHAKE IT OFF
7. FATHER FIGURE
8. THE BLACK DOG
9. STAY STAY STAY

## P.57

```
V L H E O N S T Q B E J B O
D D A R F P Y G R G L R E P
S O H I G H S C H O O L J A
Q W W G M I P N D S M Q E L
U I G N B E H A Q W L T W I
P S J E B V T R O C J J E T
R H A K L A W O F Y U O L E
E L D E S T D A U G H T E R
N I J I M M G A D F Y S D E
T S N B K Z A Y B N R O W C
O T F A O F O R T N I G H T
S P R A Z V C T O C B E P D
K M R C L A R A B O W V Z A
A N T I H E R O H O N N D H
```

## P.66

**CLUE:** Heard you calling on this!
**ANSWER:**
The Fate of Ophelia

**CLUE:** A gem made in the lightning strikes.
**ANSWER:**
Opalite

**CLUE:** You can eat it if you want!
**ANSWER:**
Honey

**CLUE:** These lovely flowers belong to Kitty.
**ANSWER:**
The Life of a Showgirl

## P.45

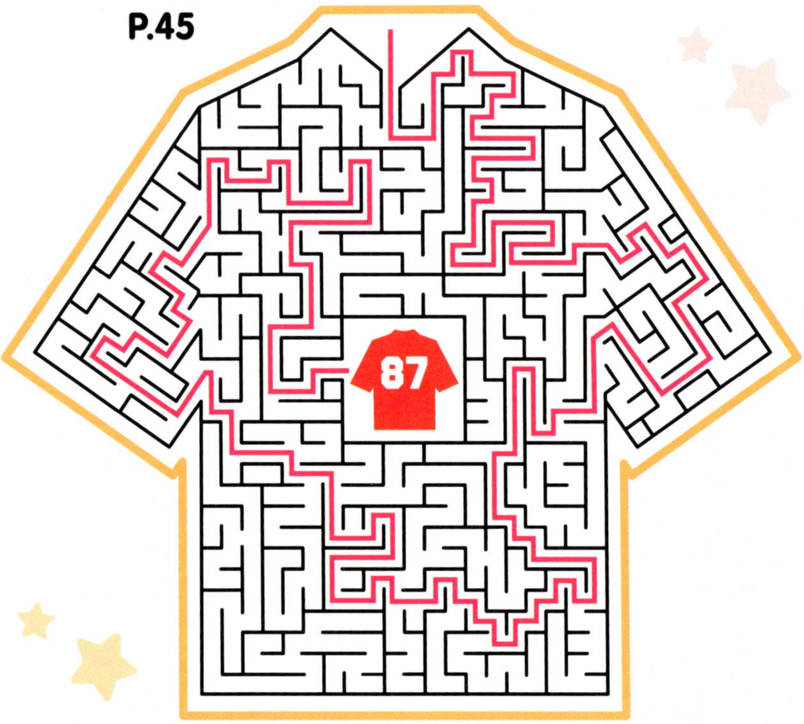

# CREDITS:

**Front cover:** PICTURES: Alamy Images, ZUMA Press, Inc.
**5:** PICTURES: Alamy Images, Image Press Agency
**6–7:** PICTURES: Alamy Images, Image Press Agency / Shutterstock, Featureflash Photo Agency / Alamy Images, Australian Associated Press / Alamy Images, Thomas Jackson
**8–9:** WORDS: X, @tswifterastour: The Eras Tour, 24th September 2023
PICTURES: Shutterstock, Everett Collection / Shutterstock / Shutterstock, Jaclyn Vernace / Shutterstock, s_bukley / Shutterstock, Joe Seer / Alamy Images, Associated Press
**10–11:** PICTURES: Shutterstock, Everett Collection / Shutterstock, s_bukley / Shutterstock: Featureflash Photo Agency / Shutterstock, Debby Wong / Shutterstock, Erman Gunes / Alamy Images, PA Images / Alamy Images, Raj Valley
**12–13:** PICTURES: Shutterstock, Featureflash Photo Agency / Shutterstock, Erman Gunes / Shutterstock, Graham Drew Photography / Shutterstock, rblfmr
**14–15:** PICTURES: Alamy Images, Associated Press / Alamy Images, Patti McConville / Alamy Images, Thomas Jackson
**16–17:** PICTURES: Shutterstock, DJSully / Shutterstock, Featureflash Photo Agency / Shutterstock, Sodel Vladyslav / Alamy Images, MediaPunch Inc / Alamy Images, Australian Associated Press
**18–19:** WORDS: Instagram, @sabrinacarpenter: Sabrina Carpenter, 13th August 2025
PICTURES: Alamy Images, Thomas Jackson / Shutterstock, Fred Duval / Alamy Images, PA Images
**20–21:** WORDS: YouTube, New Heights podcast: Taylor Swift, 13th August 2025
PICTURES: Shutterstock, Ben Houdijk / Alamy Images, AFF
**22–23:** PICTURES: YouTube, Disney Plus, 'Taylor Swift The End of an Era Official Trailer Disney+' trailer
**24–25:** PICTURES: Alamy Images, Associated Press / Alamy Images, Sharon Dobson
**26–27:** WORDS: 'Anti-Hero', Taylor Swift
PICTURES: YouTube, Taylor Swift, 'The Fate of Ophelia' music video / YouTube, Taylor Swift, 'cardigan' music video / YouTube, Taylor Swift, 'Opalite' music video / YouTube, Taylor Swift, 'You Need To Calm Down' music video / YouTube, Taylor Swift, 'Bad Blood' music video / YouTube, Taylor Swift, 'Love Story' music video
**28–29:** PICTURES: Alamy Images, Associated Press / Alamy Images, ZUMA Press, Inc.
**30–31:** PICTURES: Alamy Images, Sipa US / Alamy Images, Thomas Jackson / Alamy Images, WENN Rights Ltd / Alamy Images, Tsuni / USA / Alamy Images, ZUMA Press, Inc.
**32–33:** PICTURES: Alamy Images, UPI / Alamy Images, Thomas Jackson / Shutterstock, A.PAES
**34–35:** WORDS: New Heights podcast, episode 58: Travis Kelce, 11th October 2023
PICTURES: Alamy Images, Everett Collection Inc / Shutterstock, Ringo Chiu / Alamy Images, Stephen Chung / Alamy Images, Image Press Agency / Shutterstock, PJ McDonnell / Shutterstock, Andrew Leyden
**36–37:** WORDS: Taylor Swift, The Eras Tour
PICTURES: Shutterstock, Tinseltown / Alamy Images, Associated Press / Alamy Images, LaPresse
**38–39:** PICTURES: Alamy Images, Album / Alamy Images, UPI / Alamy Images, EQRoy / Alamy Images, Associated Press / Alamy Images, MediaPunch Inc
**40–41:** WORDS: Taylor Swift, NYU Commencement Speech, 18th May 2022 / The Tonight Show Starring Jimmy Fallon: Taylor Swift, 6th October 2025
PICTURES: YouTube, Taylor Swift, '22' music video / Shutterstock, Everett Collection / Alamy Images, Guy Corbishley / Alamy Images, MediaPunch Inc / Alamy Images, Associated Press / Alamy Images, AFF / YouTube, Taylor Swift, 'Look What You Made Me Do' music video
**42–43:** PICTURES: Alamy Images, Associated Press / Alamy Images, ZUMA Press, Inc / Shutterstock, Kathy Hutchins
**44:** PICTURES: Alamy Images, Richard Saker
**46–47:** PICTURES: Alamy Images, Associated Press / Alamy Images, PictureLux / The Hollywood Archive / Alamy Images, Imaginechina Limited
**48–49:** PICTURES: Alamy Images, Imagespace / Alamy Images, Sipa US / Alamy Images, Francesca Sara Cauli / Alamy Images, ZUMA Press, Inc.
**50–51:** PICTURES: Alamy Images, ZUMA Press, Inc. / Alamy Images, Associated Press
**52–53:** PICTURES: Alamy Images, AFF / Alamy Images, Tsuni / USA / Alamy Images, WENN Rights Ltd / Alamy Images, Suzan Moore / Alamy Images, Sam Kovak / Alamy Images, Jason Richardson / Alamy Images, MediaPunch Inc / Alamy Images, Sipa US / Alamy Images, PA Images / Alamy Images, Thomas Jackson / YouTube, Taylor Swift, 'The Fate of Ophelia' music video
**54–55:** PICTURES: Alamy Images, Associated Press / Alamy Images, Bang Media International / Alamy Images, Newscom
**58–59:** PICTURES: Alamy Images, The Photo Access / Alamy Images, Sipa US / Alamy Images, Everett Collection Inc
**60–61:** WORDS: The Washington Post: Taylor Swift, 20th October 2022
PICTURES: YouTube, Taylor Swift, 'The Man' music video / YouTube, Taylor Swift, 'Bejweled' music video / YouTube, Taylor Swift, 'The Fate of Ophelia' music video / YouTube, Taylor Swift, 'cardigan' music video / YouTube, Taylor Swift, 'You Need To Calm Down' music video / YouTube, Taylor Swift, 'Anti-Hero' music video
**62–63:** PICTURES: Alamy Images, Associated Press
**64–65:** WORDS: Oxford English Dictionary, 2023
PICTURES: Alamy Images, Ben Schott / Alamy Images, Associated Press / Alamy Images, Imaginechina Limited

100% UNOFFICIAL

100% UNOFFICIAL

100% UNOFFICIAL

100% UNOFFICIAL

100% UNOFFICIAL